The World of Work

Choosing a Career in
Law Enforcement

D1487984

If you are looking for an exciting, rewarding, and steady job, the field of law enforcement might be for you.

The World of Work
Choosing a Career in Law Enforcement

Claudine G. Wirths

THE ROSEN PUBLISHING GROUP, INC.
NEW YORK

Published in 1997, 2000 by The Rosen Publishing Group, Inc.
29 East 21st Street, New York, NY 10010

Copyright © 1997, 2000 by The Rosen Publishing Group, Inc.

Revised Edition

Library of Congress Cataloging-in-Publication Data

Wirths, Claudine G.
    Choosing a career in law enforcement / Claudine G. Wirths.
       p.   cm.—(The world of work)
    Includes bibliographical references and index.
    Summary: Offers an overview of careers in law enforcement, including
police officer, security guard, and private investigator.
    ISBN 0-8239-3282-6
    1. Law enforcement—Vocational guidance—United States—Juvenile
literature. 2. Police—Vocational guidance—United States—Juvenile
literature. [1. Law enforcement—Vocational guidance. 2. Police—
Vocational guidance. 3. Vocational guidance. 4. Occupations.]
I. Title. II. Series: World of work (New York, N.Y.)
HV7922.W55   1997
363.2'.3'02373—dc20   96-17626
                                                         CIP
                                                         AC

Contents

Introduction

At some point in your day, you will most likely see at least one person involved in law enforcement. It may be a state trooper on her way to the interstate, a police officer walking his beat in your neighborhood, or a traffic officer writing a ticket for an illegally parked car. Other law enforcers that you might see are building security guards, park rangers, control officers picking up stray animals, and people directing traffic at school crossings. Other law enforcers, such as store theft detectives, can be more difficult to detect because they don't wear uniforms.

Although jobs within the field of law enforcement vary widely, people in these jobs tend to share certain characteristics. These include personal initiative, self-discipline, and integrity. To be successful in law enforcement, you also need to have a clear understanding of right and wrong. You must be able to act as a problem solver and to think and react quickly in a variety of situations. Leaders and strategic thinkers are also essential for successful law enforcement. Above all, you must enjoy helping people and working to improve your community.

A Little About the Law

Laws help us maintain safety, order, and peace. There are many degrees of breaking the law. A misdemeanor, a common offense, is less serious than a felony. Depending on the nature of the crime, someone who commits a misdemeanor must either pay a fine or go to jail, though never for more than one year. When a person commits a felony, like burglary or murder, he or she is punished according to the results of a trial.

These levels of breaking the law are recorded on your police record, something that stays with you throughout your life. Between the moment that a lawbreaker is caught and the time that he or she is punished for the crime, several different law enforcers are involved.

Would you guess that being a file clerk counts as a career in law enforcement? It does. File clerks, fingerprint examiners, and other people who support officers are

Most people in law enforcement have two things in common:
They respect the law, and they respect other people.

extremely important in law enforcement.
There are many law-enforcement tasks that
the police department leaves to civilian
personnel. Psychologists, chemists,
biologists, photographers, and many other
specialists can find employment with large
police departments. They are important
because their expertise can be the key to
cracking a case.

Training and Experience
Law-enforcement personnel of all levels are
needed in local government, state
government, the federal government, and

private practice. To work in any government position, you need to be a United States citizen. It is possible to obtain a job in law enforcement without a high school diploma, but unfortunately you can expect to be paid poorly and to remain in low-level positions.

The educational requirements and opportunities for advancement vary between different branches of law enforcement. Many police forces encourage their officers to pursue higher education while serving on the force. In addition, law-enforcement departments often offer in-house training for both newly-hired employees and longtime workers who want to brush up on old skills or learn new ones.

Police officers work for the municipal or city government.

Local Law-Enforcement Opportunities

1

Real-life police work can sometimes be as exciting as it looks on television, but what you don't see on television is all of the training and preparation required to become a police officer. Because law enforcement is a local concern, the path to the police force differs from community to community and from state to state. Smaller communities may require new officers to complete an apprenticeship program. Most large cities maintain police academies where aspiring officers are trained in the various aspects of police work. These trainees are called cadets. Examples of classes that cadets take while attending academies include patrol procedures, criminal law, self-defense, firearms, physical training, narcotics, and emergency driving. Cadets get to perform minor police duties, such as directing traffic.

My name is Terry, and I live in a midsize city in Maryland. I've wanted to be a police officer since I was a little kid. In high school

I didn't study hard at first. Then my dad told me that if I wanted to be a police officer I would have to finish high school, so I tried harder and finally graduated.

In my city you can join the police force as soon as you get out of high school by becoming a police cadet. That's what I decided to do. To be a regular officer on the police force where I live, you have to be twenty-one, but I didn't want to wait till then.

I first went to the municipal (city) personnel office. That's where people are hired. I filled out a lot of papers. Then I scheduled an appointment for a physical and some written exams.

The day of the exams, they really checked me out. The medical exam didn't worry me because I had passed a physical to play high school sports. I knew I was okay for police height and weight requirements, too. A bunch of other physical tests showed how well I could see and how strong and quick I was. I also took some written tests.

While I was taking these tests, they checked my record to find out if I had ever been in trouble with the police. That scared me a little because when I was ten I was caught shoplifting candy. The officer told me that since I hadn't done anything worse as I got older, that was okay. If I had been arrested for breaking into someone's house when I was sixteen, they would have rejected my application.

They tested me for drugs, and I was clean. If there had been any traces of drug use, I would have failed. They also gave me a lie detector test and asked me if I had ever used drugs or alcohol. I said I hadn't used drugs, but I had drunk beer on a few weekends. They told me that since I was telling the truth, I would pass. I was told that I would have to cut out any drinking until I was of legal age, twenty-one. They said they would check me every so often.

The police department also needed reference letters. I asked my school counselor, my minister, and some other people to write recommendations for me. They were asked whether I could be trusted and whether I stayed calm even when others around me got upset.

I also had to have no points on my driver's license, meaning that I had not been caught breaking any traffic laws.

A few weeks later I received a letter that said I was in!

As a police cadet I didn't make much money, but I did wear a uniform. The first thing they did was to send me back to school. Three mornings a week I went with other cadets to the police academy, where we learned about the laws of our city. As a cadet, I couldn't make arrests. Instead I washed patrol cars, made lists of what officers brought in after arrests, and even helped on a sting.

A sting is an undercover operation, so I wasn't in uniform at the time. I was sent into a store to buy wine. Two officers outside the store watched, but they stood where the cashier couldn't see them. Because the clerk sold me wine without asking to see proof of my age, he was arrested. He gave me a really dirty look and called me insulting names. But I know that he was actually angry about being caught and just trying to take it out on me.

When I turned twenty-one, I was sworn in as a police officer. At first I was on probation. That meant that I had one year to prove that I was fit to be a police officer. I had to go to the police academy for a month. That's where I really learned about using guns, controlling traffic, and lots more.

The thought of high-speed chases and catching people who have broken the law is exciting to many people.

Among other things, we had to write reports and learn how to present cases in court.

After that I went to work with an older officer. What he taught me about policing went way beyond what was covered in the course work. Sometimes we drove around in a patrol car. Other times we walked or biked around the streets. We were responsible for a specific area of our city and tried to get to know the people on our beat.

We performed lots of different jobs. We directed traffic, answered calls, and helped out at car accidents. Sometimes we staked out places where we thought a crime would happen. We chased speeders and ticketed people who ran through stop signs. Sometimes the work was boring, but other times it was as action-packed as it is in the movies.

That first year seemed to last a long time. There were officers I didn't like very much at first, but since I knew my life might depend on them someday, I learned to get along with them.

What don't I like about police work? I don't like the idea that I might have to kill someone someday. I don't like arresting people I know. That happens sometimes. I also don't like having my hair cut this short. I wish I made more money, but it's steady work and I'm not likely to be laid off. After a couple of years I can make more money, if I pass the tests and move up in rank.

What do I like? I like night-shift work. I like working when everyone else is asleep. I'm glad that people sleep more safely because of me. Being outdoors a lot is great, too. So is working with a partner. And I like the exciting times when the station is alive with everyone working on a big case. I guess I like being where the action is!

Terry's story is typical in many ways of the beginning career of a police officer. Of

As a police officer, you may have to do some jobs that you don't like, such as arresting someone you know.

course, police work is not exactly the same in all parts of the country. Some areas hire officers as young as age nineteen. In general, small towns pay less than big cities. Some cities want new employees to have attended college for at least one year. A felony conviction on an applicant's record usually results in disqualification, but in a few cities you can have a felony on your record as long as it is not within the last five years. Convictions for crimes and offenses are evaluated during a background investigation.

Upon retirement, police officers receive a pension. Since they often retire quite young,

many former officers find work providing
private security for corporations or individuals.

Other Areas of Local Law Enforcement

Deputy sheriffs, who have to pass the same
tests as officers, work for the county instead
of the city. Sometimes they serve as the
police for a rural county. They patrol, make
arrests, deliver important papers, guard the
courthouse, and take prisoners to court.

Jailers work at city or county jails. They
learn their work on the job. Most of the
prisoners in these jails have committed lesser
crimes and serve shorter sentences. Jailers
check prisoners in; take care of their
belongings; give them food, sheets, towels,
and clothes; and keep records on them. The
longer a jailer works, the higher the pay.

Court deputies keep order in county
courthouses. They also stand by to make
sure that the jury is chosen correctly, that the
jurors are fed, and that they are prevented
from talking with members of the public. If
the jurors have to stay overnight in a hotel,
court deputies often help guard them. Other
common duties of court deputies include
working with the court clerk, the person who

maintains the court's records, and making sure that trials are held in the correct rooms. Court deputies attend police classes and receive on-the-job training.

Dispatchers answer emergency phones and send help when needed. Dispatchers must be good at handling many jobs at once. Sometimes they get five or six calls simultaneously and have to decide how to handle all of them. They must pass written tests, speak clearly, keep cool in a crisis, and know how to use a computer. Training may be on the job or part of a special program.

Other Local Government Jobs

If a county has a county police system as well as sheriffs, county police handle most of the crime work and traffic control. Transportation guards watch television monitors to check for problems on elevators or on platforms of subway systems. Finally, animal control officers pick up stray animals and enforce animal laws. Port wardens enforce laws at ports.

State Government Law Enforcement

2

M*y name is Donnell, and I'm a guard at a state prison. My official title is corrections officer. Just before I turned twenty-one, I lost my job at the supermarket. So I applied at the state personnel office for a job at the prison. I passed a short test that showed I could read and follow directions. I passed the physical, too, but it was tough. I wished I had exercised more before I took it.*

I soon found out that this is no easy job. I went to school for three months right in the prison. We learned how to talk to prisoners, how to care for guns, and how to shoot to kill. I learned how to defend myself if someone jumps me. I also learned how to hold a prisoner who is violent and how to handle riots.

I was scared at first when I realized that some of the people in my prison are murderers and muggers. But I found that many of the prisoners are not as different from your average citizen as I thought.

I work an eight-hour day, but I have to be ready to work whenever they need me. Last year I had to work New Year's Eve even though it wasn't my shift.

The starting pay isn't bad. I'll be a sergeant next year if I pass the tests. I will make more money and live on the prison grounds. The state will provide a house and health care for me and my family.

My advice is, don't go into this job unless it interests you. The work requires lots of patience and you need to be smart and strong. I have to stay calm if someone murders someone in my area. I have to help inmates understand legal work. I listen to them when someone in their family dies. I provide their supplies—toothpaste, soap, toilet paper. I have to keep my temper, even when an inmate yells at me. At the same time, I must be ready at any second to defend my life. The rewarding part is that I give help to people who really need it. I'm glad I took the job.

Pay scales vary in different prisons, but the training, working conditions, and duties are basically the same in both state and federal prisons. If you're interested in this tough but rewarding job, check out the prison nearest you.

Other State Jobs in Law Enforcement

There are other state-funded positions in law enforcement that may interest you. Most of these jobs require at least a high school diploma. To find out more about them, inquire at the state personnel office.

State patrol officers have almost the same duties as city police, but they may have to work in various parts of the state. The state is usually divided into districts called barracks. An officer can be sent to work at any barrack.

Many places have a cadet program. If candidates pass physical and psychological tests, they can enter the program right out of high school. Cadets receive on-the-job training and spend their time performing tasks such as weighing trucks. Unless they fail as cadets, these people are hired as full-time officers when they turn twenty-one. Before beginning work as full-time patrol officers, they go to school for several weeks to learn about the laws of the state and about gun use and safety.

The job of the state patrol is to enforce state laws. State patrol officers often help to protect the governor and other state officials and work with park rangers to enforce laws

Highway patrol officers enforce the laws governing road travel.

in parks and forests. They also answer local calls for help and help out at crime scenes.

In addition, state patrol officers control traffic on state and interstate roads and help at accidents. They must be good at writing reports and testifying in court. These officers need to stay physically fit, as the work can be tiring. At times they may have to drive for hours. By passing various tests, an officer can be promoted and make more money.

Highway patrol officers handle traffic in most states. They often have limited police powers. Their job is to enforce speed laws, handle accidents, and help motorists in trouble. They take tests similar to those taken by state patrol officers.

For natural resources police officers, outdoor areas are their regular beat. Natural resources officers, who work closely with park and forest rangers, must meet the same age and educational requirements as state patrol officers. They may also have to learn to ride a horse, pilot a boat, or drive a snowmobile. Duties include checking on gaming licenses, policing public campsites, and generally protecting forests and parks.

Natural resources police officers must be able to work in all types of weather and to

Fingerprint classifiers are careful, detail-oriented people.

lift heavy objects, run after suspects, and handle physically dangerous situations such as climbing cliffs, crawling through caves, or even crossing deserts. These officers often patrol alone and must be ready to work whenever they are needed.

Crime lab technicians help solve crimes by studying evidence from crime scenes. Responsibilities include matching bullets to guns, verifying handwriting on documents, and going to the scene of a wreck to study a car's tire tracks. Crime lab technicians need to be detail-oriented and good with cameras and lab equipment and should enjoy science.

Since they often testify in court, they must be able to write a good report and speak well in public. Becoming a technician usually requires at least one year of college.

Are you good at details? Do you like keeping records? Do you make very few errors in your work? If so, fingerprint classifier may be the job for you. Large state crime labs hire people whose only responsibilities are to classify and compare fingerprints all day. There are also jobs for fingerprint experts within the federal government. These jobs are not action-packed, but the work is crucial. Someone's life may depend on your finding the right fingerprint. If this field interests you, you need to take courses in criminal justice, computers, and photography.

Lifeguards enforce rules and protect public property. They often work part-time, though in some states the job is full-time. Lifeguards may work at an indoor pool in a state park or outside at a pool, lake, or beach.

Lifeguarding may also be a local government job. Lifeguards must be in good health and have to pass first-aid and life-saving tests.

Other Job Prospects in Your State

Fire wardens watch for forest fires, enforce fire laws, and help extinguish fires. Park rangers protect visitors and enforce state laws in parks. Bailiffs keep order in courtrooms.

Just by looking around your state, you will find there are jobs in courthouses, parks, and forests. Don't forget to look at United States and Canadian government jobs, too.

Park rangers are law-enforcement officers in the national parks.

Federal Government Opportunities 3

My badge reads S. Grissom. The S stands for Sandra, but everyone calls me Sandy. As a park ranger, I'm a law-enforcement officer in a national park. I like being outside—rain or shine, hot or cold. Many parks need law-enforcement people.

In general, the National Park Service wants you to be good at something besides law enforcement. That can be history, wildflowers, rescue work, or something else. I got my job because I went to a two-year college and I know a lot about fish. I worked at the park every summer, and that helped me get the job, too.

To be a ranger I had to be twenty-one and pass oral and written tests and a medical exam. Once hired, I went to a training program to learn park rules and my duties. I was sent to a school called the Federal Law Enforcement Training Center (FLETC) for six weeks.

Schoolwork was easier for the rangers who had college degrees, but I worked hard and passed. We learned criminal, civil, and traffic laws as well as park and forest laws. We learned to use and care for guns. We wrote reports and practiced public speaking. We even learned to fight forest fires.

Most park visitors obey the laws, but there are always some troublemakers. Once we arrested a man who had set fire to a campground. Some drug dealers hid out in our forest, too, and I helped capture them. In some parks, the rangers help the local police. In my park we're the only police. We do everything.

Mostly I give talks to school kids about the fish in our lake. During talks, I don't wear a gun. When I'm on patrol I wear a bulletproof vest and carry a gun. I don't like wearing body armor because it's heavy and not made for women, but I wear it to be safe.

To be good at a job like mine, you have to stay alert. You must make quick decisions. You have to be able to shift quickly from talking about wildflowers to looking for an illegal hunter.

Every year I go to training programs for a few days. We learn about changes in the laws and new rules for the parks and forests. Even after ten years I wouldn't trade my job for any other. I know that my work helps keep our park safe for everyone. I get to help save the forests and parks.

Currently, most park and forest rangers are expected to be law-enforcement officers. Check with the park and forest department in your state as well as the National Park Service for jobs. In these jobs you may work alone or you may be in a park with thousands of visitors. You may be sent to other parks as you move up. In addition to getting along well with other people, you must be good at planning and carrying out your work.

Other Federal Law-Enforcement Jobs

Most of the following federal government jobs require at least a high school diploma.

Building guards don't need experience to begin working. However, a veteran of the armed forces, such as the Army, Navy, Air Force, or Marines, stands the best chance of being hired. Guards are sent to school to learn to handle guns. They learn other duties on the job. Some guards sit or stand at the entrances of government buildings. They check photo badges to be sure that visitors have a right to be there. They also check people entering the building for concealed guns or bombs.

Other guards patrol buildings. They answer questions and give directions. Night-shift guards walk through the building to ensure that doors, windows, and files are locked or closed. They also watch for fires and for people who should not be in the building. Many guards are on their feet all the time, which can be very tiring. The work is steady. There is not much chance to advance, but you can expect good health care, vacations, and a retirement plan.

Border patrol officers often work alone and must be able to make good decisions independently. Officers check roads, trains, planes, and boats to find people who enter the country illegally. Because some of these people are dangerous, officers often risk their lives.

This is not a job for someone who doesn't want to study and work hard. To be in the border patrol you must pass tough physical, written, and oral tests. Once hired, you are

Customs workers make sure that illegal items, such as drugs or weapons, don't enter or leave the country.

sent to FLETC or to the Border Patrol Academy for five months to learn law enforcement and Spanish. Examples of the classes that you take at either school include immigration and nationality law, border patrol operations, the care and use of firearms, and defensive driving techniques. After you graduate, you will receive twenty-four weeks of on-the-job training.

Border patrol work is hard on family life. The officers are often away from home for long periods of time. They may be sent anywhere along the Canadian or Mexican border or on either coast. Families may have to move many times. But like other U.S. government employees, border patrol officers receive good benefits.

Customs workers are hired to work at places of entry into the United States. These could be airports, docks, or border crossings. Customs workers carry out the laws concerning what may leave or enter the country. They check for drugs or other illegal items, such as stolen cars or goods that someone might try to sneak out. They also collect duties (taxes) from tourists for certain items bought in other countries.

You need to be twenty-one to become a customs officer, and it helps if you know at least two languages. It also helps to know a lot about traveling and tourism because this knowledge may give you an edge in detecting risks and theft and identifying taxable items. Customs officers work in shifts, usually eight hours at a time, either during the day or at night. The work can be dangerous, as it may require dealing with people who are involved in illegal activities.

If you like the ocean and boats, consider a job with the Coast Guard, a military service that enforces the laws of the sea and rescues people in danger out at sea. To be hired you

Joining the armed services is one way to enter the field of law enforcement.

must be between seventeen and twenty-seven and have at least a high school education. You also need to pass the physical, as well as the Armed Services Vocational Aptitude Battery (ASVAB), a test that everyone must take to join the armed services. If accepted, you will be sent to basic training for eight weeks and then sent to a Coast Guard unit. In that unit you will train for an additional twelve to twenty-four weeks to learn a specific skill, such as boating. After that you will be assigned to a unit that needs your skills. You can retire after twenty years with a good retirement package.

Postal police officers must be twenty-one and physically fit to apply. They need to have good hearing and good eyesight. They must be able to read and write well, get along well with people, and pass a written test.

Many people think that the federal government runs the post office. In truth, the post office is privately run, but it shares many of the federal government job benefits. Postal police officers secure post offices, both inside and outside. They may work at the loading docks where postal trucks park, or they may sit inside the post office, checking badges of people who enter the mailroom. Check the bulletin board at your local post office for current job openings.

Other U.S. Government Jobs

Immigration guards watch over immigrants until they are admitted to the United States or sent back to their own country.

The U.S. Army and U.S. Navy train people to be military police. Many law-enforcement jobs give preference to veterans. As a result, being in any of the services is a good way to start a career in law enforcement.

If you don't like working for a government agency, you will find that many private businesses hire law-enforcement people. In addition, if you cannot work for the government because you have a police record, working for a private business may be the solution. If you can show that you have changed your ways and can prove your dependability, companies may be willing to hire you despite your record.

Law Enforcement in Private Companies

4

My name is Marissa and I am a mall security guard. I love my job. It is my responsibility to make sure that shoppers are safe here. I had no idea how many facets there are to this job when I applied for it over a year ago. I thought that it would be an easy after-school job, but I ended up learning so much that I stayed on as weekend help.

A good percentage of the people who come here are here to shop. I went through special training to help me spot the people who are here to steal or cause harm to others. You can't always tell who the troublemakers are, so sometimes you just have to be patient and observe. Sometimes store owners will call me into their stores because they see someone suspicious or have actually caught a thief. I am not allowed to arrest someone because I am not a police officer, but I am allowed to detain, or hold, a person until the police arrive. I act as a witness and tell the police what I have observed. There are three mall security guards on each shift, so in emergencies we end up helping each other out.

All of the guards have different backgrounds. Some of them didn't need as much training as I did. Since my only previous related experience was working as a crossing guard, I had to undergo a good deal of training. I was trained in self-defense; how to avoid violent confrontations; how to calm people in distress, such as a lost child; and how to call for assistance. I also received first-aid training and learned what to do in weather-related emergencies.

A mall is a large area with community bathrooms and stairwells. I patrol these areas often because you never know where trouble might be lurking. The mall is also a popular hangout for kids and sometimes I have to break up groups of rowdy teens. When the movies get out, I make it a point to stand by the ropes to help clear any crowded areas. When people are behaving in an unsafe manner, I tell them to stop. If they don't obey, I ask them to leave.

Sometimes people get sick or injured at the mall. It is my job to assist them and make sure that they get the help and medical attention that they need.

I have worked the night shift a few times. On the night shift I made sure that all the doors and windows were locked after closing time. I checked that everybody was out of the mall and that the bathrooms and stairwells were clear. I escorted employees to their cars if they felt that they needed protection.

Since walking is part of my job, I never feel as if I have nothing to do. I walk my route, say hello to store owners and familiar faces, and keep an eye out for anyone who might need me. I hope to work here for a few more years and then perhaps look into joining the police force.

Most malls hire security guards and night guards. They want people who are neat, responsible, and hardworking. Night workers are more likely to face dangerous situations because there are fewer people around to help.

The most important part of the job is dealing with the public. The mall wants workers who get along with others and who will help the public first and enforce rules second. There are no particular educational requirements for security guards, although a high school diploma usually helps.

Some large malls in high-crime areas do not hire security guards like Marissa. Instead, they hire off-duty police officers.

Other Private Jobs

Store theft detectives are hired by large stores, both in malls and out. The guards wear everyday clothes and walk around the store looking for shoplifters and watching clerks to be sure that they don't steal.

Some stores have automatic alarms that sound when someone tries to take something out of the store without paying for it. The store security guard stops the person and asks to examine his or her packages. Guards have to be polite because the customer may have paid for the item and sounded the alarm because the clerk forgot to remove the tag.

Private investigators (PIs), or private eyes, are hired by people to investigate a situation. Typical assignments include searching for someone who has run away, trying to discover whether an employee is

Security guards must always be alert and aware of what's going on around them.

stealing from his or her boss, or obtaining proof (usually photographs) for a client that his or her spouse is having an affair. A good PI must be curious, write well, and have a good memory. New employees start at a little over minimum wage, but after a few years can earn a good salary. Most states require PIs to have no police record and to take a special course if they are going to carry a gun.

Some agencies send new hires out with a more experienced PI to be trained, though the best agencies look for employees who have already received some training at a school for private investigators. Most of these schools help their students find jobs after graduation. These schools have a high dropout rate because many people, once they begin training, find that they do not like the work.

Be sure that the private investigation company you want to work for has a state license. You could get into trouble with the law if your company does not have one.

Night watch workers guard businesses at night. Most business owners hire people who have already worked as security guards. This is a job for someone who can stay awake at night, enjoys working alone, and is not afraid of potentially dangerous situations. Some night watch workers need to be able to work with a guard dog. No special training is needed for this position unless the particular job requires carrying a gun.

Airport security personnel check luggage and people for weapons, drugs, and other illegal items prior to boarding and try to spot suspicious-looking passengers. These workers are hired by the company that runs the airport. They need to have good people skills and must be able to spot troublemakers and to work without letting others distract or hurry them. Airport security workers receive instruction on using metal detectors and X-ray machines and on what to look for in luggage and packages.

Armored car drivers and guards are men and women who transport money to and from banks. They are hired by security companies or banks. Armored car drivers and guards are trained to carry and handle weapons. They rarely face danger, although people occasionally try to steal money from the cars. This is a job for people who can stay alert even when nothing much is happening, which is most of the time.

Security agency workers are hired by some companies part-time for small security jobs. To do this you need to be adaptable. In one job you might control traffic or the crowd at a music concert. In another job you might have to guard gifts at a wedding reception. Beginning workers receive minimum wage. Many of these companies go out of business in a short time, so if you are interested in doing this kind of work, look for a company that has been around for a while.

Airport security personnel are responsible for making sure no weapons or illegal items are brought onto airplanes.

Bodyguards are hired to protect celebrities, politicians, and other people whose lives could be in danger. Bodyguards must be strong and fit, and if they carry a gun, they need a license. Gate tenders sit at gates of private homes or businesses. They let in only the people who are on a list. Campus police are hired by colleges to provide security on the grounds of the college.

Preparation for Law-Enforcement Jobs

5

Take a look at these questions before you decide for sure that a career in law enforcement is right for you:

- **Do you obey the law?** Answering yes means that you don't do drugs, steal, or have a bad driving record. Your teachers and other adults see you as someone they can trust. You can still have fun, hang out with friends, join clubs, and belong to a sports team—just don't spend your weekends drinking alcohol and getting into trouble. Almost every job in law enforcement will be closed to you if you have a serious offense on your record after age sixteen.
- **Do you stay fit?** You must be healthy and strong for law-enforcement work.
- **Do you read newspapers or magazines at least once a week?** Most law-enforcement jobs require you to read well and to understand what you read.

- **Do you write well?** Almost all law enforcement jobs require writing reports.
- **Do you know how to use a computer?** Every police department will soon be using computers.
- **Are you academically prepared for a law-enforcement job?** Some useful classes are psychology, sociology, law, and science, as well as courses in marriage and the family, as police are often called to break up family fights.

If you think a law-enforcement career might be right for you, here are other ways to prepare yourself. This preparation can help you gain experience that could lead to a job in law enforcement.

- Volunteer to help with neighborhood watch programs. Take your turn patrolling the neighborhood and reporting any trouble to the police.
- Take courses in martial arts or other self-defense techniques. Being able to defend yourself without a gun is great training.
- Take a defensive driving course. Some places offer classes that teach you how to drive under dangerous conditions.
- Attend DARE (Drug Abuse Resistance Education) meetings, ride-along

programs, and junior police, police club, and other programs offered by police. These opportunities give you a firsthand look at police as people.

- Take first-aid, lifesaving, and CPR courses. Such courses will prepare you to help in emergencies.
- Learn a second language. Since many people in the United States do not speak English, knowing another language is often a big plus when applying for a job.
- Volunteer for jobs that involve working with people. Lots of jobs in your school and community can get you working with people of all ages and types. Check out what you can do in a local hospital, fire station, or place of worship.

The Next Step

Now that you have learned more about jobs in the field of law enforcement, you may have decided whether law enforcement seems right for you.

If you have concluded that law-enforcement work is not for you, don't panic! No one should go into law enforcement—or any field—unless it is right for him or her. You will find something eventually. Keep looking.

If you have decided that you like the idea of police work, but haven't found the right job within the field, don't give up. Look for a job that involves helping the police. These jobs include secretary, file clerk, cleaning person, and maintenance worker. All of these jobs require you to pass tests specific to the job and to have a clean police record.

In small towns and counties you may be able to get one of these jobs by talking directly to the chief of police or sheriff. In larger cities you must apply for one of these positions through the regular personnel office. Once hired, you can request a transfer to a department that you prefer as soon as there is an opening. The police will tell you that the people who do these jobs are a great help. If you do your job well, you can be sure that you are doing important work for law enforcement.

If you think you have found a job that looks right for you, it's time to take action! Contact some of the places listed in the next chapter to get more information about that job. Talk to people who do that job and ask them to tell you more about it. Then you'll be ready to apply for the job yourself.

Applying for Law-Enforcement Jobs

6

If you are seeking a local government job, turn to the blue pages of the telephone book to find the number of your municipal or county personnel office. Call and ask how to find out which jobs are open and what you need to do to apply. You can also check under the heading Employment Service in the list of the Frequently Called Numbers at the front of your telephone book.

If a state government job appeals to you, look up the number of your state personnel office in the blue pages. Also check under Job Line—Employment Service Information in the white pages. Call and ask about finding out what jobs are open, what you need to do to apply for them, and what the educational requirements are for the positions.

If you want a federal government job, look in the blue pages for a federal job information center. If one is not listed, dial the operator and ask for the number in your state. At that number they can tell you about job openings, what you need to do to get the jobs, and the educational requirements.

For information on becoming a postal police officer, check your local post office's bulletin board.

To find out about opportunities in private businesses and industry, start at your state personnel office. Call and ask for information about the kind of job that interests you.

Many cities and counties also offer job-hunting help. Ask a high school counselor if your town provides special help.

Résumé Tips

Believe it or not, preparing a résumé can be fun. Basically, you get to make yourself look as good as possible without stretching the truth.

A successful résumé should be something that showcases the best qualities of yourself and your past experience. Your résumé should summarize your qualifications as someone who is interested in the law enforcement field. Try thinking of your résumé as an advertisement for why someone in law enforcement would want to hire you. Emphasize jobs or experiences that show your honesty and your ability to handle responsibility.

Since the résumé is often the first thing potential employers look at when considering a candidate for a job, it is important to avoid common résumé mistakes. Certain errors are immediate signals to employers that the candidate is not detail-oriented. These include missing dates, inaccurate phone numbers and addresses, typing and spelling errors, and incorrect or vague statements. You should also avoid listing hobbies or interests that conflict with the high standards expected from someone interested in law enforcement.

Interview Tips

When an employer calls you to schedule an interview, feel good that you have made it this far. If you were honest on your résumé your interview shouldn't be too tricky or difficult.

Any interview will proceed more easily if you bring a few key items. These include extra copies of your résumé, pens and pencils, a notebook, and a list of references.

Take your time getting ready for the interview. Practice good posture for a few days before the interview, and think about possible questions that you may be asked and how to best answer them. When you meet your interviewer, remember: He or she went through the exact same thing you are going through now. Don't put so much emphasis on the interview that you forget to enjoy yourself a little. Interviews are great opportunities to casually sell yourself to an employer. At the beginning and end of the interview, shake the person's hand firmly and give a nice, comfortable smile.

Your interviewer will want to get to know as much about you as possible, but he or she is not supposed to ask you about certain subjects, such as your religious beliefs. Be sure to prepare for tough questions and to bring proper identification if necessary. If you are applying to be a police officer, for example, you will need to prove your age.

Answer all questions honestly. Take time to think about phrasing your answer instead of blurting out whatever comes to mind first. Don't assume that long silences are necessarily a bad sign; they may be tests to see if you rattle easily under pressure.

Some good "don'ts" to remember are not discussing money during the first interview and not begging for the job. Some places might not be hiring at the time that you visit them, so don't expect to land a position right away, especially if you are only there for an information-gathering interview.

A great "do" is to follow up with a note or a quick call to thank your interviewer for his or her time and consideration and to express your continued interest in the position.

One thing to remember is that no matter how great your interview goes, you can be disqualified or fired from law-enforcement positions if you are untruthful or if you intentionally withhold information on any application, interview, or paperwork associated with the position. You can also be dismissed if you are caught cheating on any examination or testing associated with the position.

Finding Part-Time Work

Some cities hire civilians for certain jobs, such as crossing guard. Your local police department can give you an idea of available positions that you can apply for that fit well with your interests and previous experience.

Call the personnel departments of the companies you would like to work for to find out about job openings.

Almost all newspaper classified sections list part-time job openings. You can look under security guards, store help, and drivers, though it is best to skim through all of the classifieds, since headings can be misleading. Another alternative is to call agencies listed under Guard & Patrol Services in the yellow pages. If you are interested in detective work, call private detective agencies and ask if they need part-time help.

A great way to find more information is to use a search engine on the Web. There are many job listings posted on Internet sites relating to careers in law enforcement. If your city has its own Web site, look for jobs under headings related to your local police force or law-enforcement divisions.

If you need to take an exam to apply for a job, ask your librarian to help you find publications in your library to help you study. One helpful publisher is Arco. They publish handbooks containing examples of what police and civil service exams are like.

Job hunting can be very time-consuming. It is normal to have to apply to more than one place before you get a job. You may even need to work another job while you hunt for a job in law enforcement.

Don't be in a hurry to hear from an agency to which you have applied. Many places check out your background before they let you know if they want to hire you. If you have not heard three weeks after your interview, call and ask politely if they are still hiring and if they are still considering you for the position. If they say no, apply to other agencies.

Let everyone know that you are job hunting. Tell your neighbors, friends, and teachers, and tell them to spread the word. The more people who know you are interested, the more likely you are to hear about a job opening.

If you really want to work in law enforcement, wait for the right job. You will spend many years of your life working, so you may as well work at something you like. If and when you do find a law-enforcement job that is right for you, you'll have the opportunity to make the world a safer place.

Glossary

Armed Services Vocational Aptitude Battery (ASVAB) Written test required for entry into all the armed services.

armored car Bulletproof truck made to carry money and other valuables.

beat The area that a police officer patrols.

body armor Bulletproof shirt worn by some law-enforcement officers.

cadet Person in training to become a police officer.

CPR Cardiopulmonary resuscitation; a method of keeping a person's heart pumping and lungs breathing.

criminal Someone who breaks a law.

enforce To uphold.

Federal Law Enforcement Training Center (FLETC) School where nearly all federal law-enforcement workers with any police power are sent to be trained.

felony Serious crime; punishment involves court appearances.

inmate Anyone held in a jail or prison.

interstate roads Main highways that pass through more than one state within the United States.

license Certification provided by the state for a person to undertake an activity.

limited police power Authority for a law-enforcement officer to enforce only certain laws.

minimum wage Standard amount of pay set by the federal government.

misdemeanor Crime less serious than a felony.

offender Someone who the police suspect has broken a law or who is arrested for a crime.

personnel office Employment office.

physical or physical exam Test done by a doctor or nurse to examine your health.

rank Position.

shoplifter Anyone who intentionally takes anything from a store without paying for it.

stake out When police officers observe a specific location in anticipation of a crime or the arrival of a suspect.

For Further Reading

Cohen, Paul, and Shari Cohen. *Careers in Law Enforcement and Security*. New York: Rosen Publishing Group, 1995.

Cuomo, George. *A Couple of Cops: On the Street, in the Crime Lab*. New York: Random House, 1995.

Gartner, Bob. *Careers in the National Parks*. Rev. ed. New York: Rosen Publishing Group, 1996.

Greenberg, Keith Elliot, and Jeanne Vestal. *Adolescent Rights: Are Young People Equal Under the Law?* Brookfield, CT: Twenty-First Century Books, 1995.

Kronenwetter, Michael. *The FBI and Law Enforcement Agencies of the United States (American Government in Action)*. Springfield, NJ: Enslow Publishers, Inc., 1997.

Mahoney, Thomas. *Law Enforcement Careers Planning*. Springfield, IL: C.C. Thomas, 1989.

Silverstein, Herma. *Threads of Evidence: Using Forensic Science to Solve Crimes*. Brookfield, CT: Twenty-First Century Books, 1996.

For More Information

For lists of all city and state police departments, call:
Knight Line USA
(800) 738-4823
(Note: There is a fee for these lists.)

In the United States
American Correctional Association (ACA)
8025 Laurel Lakes Court
Laurel, MD 20707-5075
(301) 918-1800

American Federation of Government Employees
80 F Street NW
Washington, DC 20001
(202) 737-8700

American Federation of State, County and
Municipal Employees
1625 L Street NW
Washington, DC 20036
(202) 429-1000

International Association of Chiefs of Police
515 North Washington Street

Alexandria, VA 22314
(703) 243-6500

United States Coast Guard
(410) 768-5454
Web site: http://www.uscg.mil

For information about the United States Army, Navy, or Marines, you can also check at local recruiting offices.

Web Sites

U.S. Border Patrol
http://www.usbp.com

http://www.law-enforcement.com

http://www.crisnet.com (Go to LE links for state-by-state law enforcement agencies.)

http://www.lejobs.com

http://www.officer.com

Index

About the Author
Claudine Gibson Wirths, M.A., M.Ed, has held many positions, including adjunct professor, coordinator of a career placement program for students with severe learning disabilities, and elementary school science teacher. Ms. Wirths has also served as a research consultant to many public and private agencies, including ten years with the Aiken, South Carolina, Police Department. She has co-authored thirteen books and several articles and monographs.

Photo Credits
Cover © Michael Lichter/ International Stock; p. 2 © Earl Dotter/ Impact Visuals; p. 8 © Clark Jones/ Impact Visuals; p. 12 © F.M. Kearney/ Impact Visuals; p. 15 © R. Tesa/ International stock; p. 17 © Bill Stanton/ International Stock; p. 23 © Phyllis Picardi/ International Stock; p. 25 © AP/ Wide World Photos; p. 28 © Stefan Lawrence/ International Stock; p. 33 © Martha Tabor/ Impact Visuals; p. 35 © Scott Thode/ International Stock; p. 42 © Miriam Romais/ Impact Visuals; p. 45 © Ryan Williams/ International Stock; p. 55 by Kim Sonsky.

Design: Erin McKenna